Journey into Joy

STATIONS OF THE RESURRECTION

ANDREW WALKER

Published in Great Britain in 2001 by
Society for Promoting Christian Knowledge
Holy Trinity Church
Marylebone Road
London NW1 4DU

ISBN: 0-281-05264-6

British Library Cataloguing-in-Publication Data

A catalogue record for this book is available from the British Library

Published in North America in 2001 by
Paulist Press
997 Macarthur Boulevard
Mahwah, New Jersey 07430
www.paulistpress.com

ISBN: 0-8091-0535-7

Designed and Typeset by Silver Fish Publishing Ltd.
Printed in Singapore

To the parish and people of St Peter's, Streatham

ACKNOWLEDGEMENTS AND SOURCES

Bible references are from The Jerusalem Bible © 1966 by Darton, Longman & Todd Ltd and Doubleday and Co. Inc.

Angelou, Maya, 'Still I Rise', in *I Shall Not be Moved*. Virago Press, London, 1990.

Burnside, John, 'The Resurrection', *in The Myth of the Twin*. Cape Poetry, London, 1992.

Chesterton, G. K., 'The Beatific Vision', in *Poems*. Burns and Oates, 1915.

Esquival, Julia, 'Threatened with Resurrection', in Parker J. Parker, *The Active Life*. Harper & Row, New York, 1982.

Hammarskjold, Dag, from *Markings*, translated by Leif Sjoberg and W. H. Auden.
Copyright © 1964 by Alfred A knopf Inc. and Faber & Faber Ltd.
Reprinted by permission of Alfred A. Knopf, a division of Random House Inc.

Kierkegaard, Søren, from *The Prayers of Kierkegaard* by P. F. Lefevre. The University of Chicago, 1956.

Mirikitani, Janice, 'Her Face', in *We, the Dangerous*. Virago Press, London, 1995.

Nayadu, Sarojini, 'In Salutation to the Eternal Peace', in the *Oxford Book of English Mystical Verse*. Clarendon Press, Oxford, 1924.

Niebuhr, Reinhold, from *Justice and Mercy*, 1974, ed. Ursula Niebuhr. Reprinted with permission of Elu estate of Reinhold Niebuhr.

Roberts, Michele, 'A Psalm for Easter', in *All the Selves I Was*. Virago Press, London, 1995.

Silk, David, *Prayers for Use at Alternative Services*. Mowbray, London.

Smith, Stevie, 'The Airy Christ', in *Selected Poems*, ed. James MacGibbon, Penguin, London, 1978.

ILLUSTRATIONS

CONTENTS

INTRODUCTION

In my years of parish experience and in conversation with other clergy I have often been struck by the contrast between the common observance of Lent and Easter.

In the case of the former it is clearly and enthusiastically marked out as a particular season in the Church's year by special observances and disciplines – courses, books, groups, boxes, devotions (like Stations of the Cross), planned abstinences. It is a season the whole Christian community is aware of and engaged in, both in church and out of it, during the week and on Sunday. Non-churchgoers are aware of it and sometimes participate in it ('No more chocolate for a while then, Vicar!').

Easter, though, is very different. Although equally a season, lasting fifty days to Lent's forty, it is almost universally treated as a one-off event. By Easter Tuesday, two days into the festival, people are usually asking, 'Did you have a nice Easter then?' as if it is all over. The season, of course, continues to be observed liturgically but beyond that there seems little in the way of support. No special courses, groups, boxes or devotions, and no one to my knowledge has ever recommended taking up something like chocolate or champagne and sticking to it religiously until Pentecost!

So I offer this adaptation of the traditional Stations of the Cross, with its mixture of scripture, reflection, poetry, prayer and illustration. All provide different ways, perhaps, to experience something of the profound and transforming joy that we can find in our risen Lord, properly encountered. These meditations attempt to help redress the balance between Lent and Easter and to recapture for the Church something of the energy and grace that lie for us in potential and which could surely make apostles of us all.

STATION I

THE DISCOVERY OF THE EMPTY TOMB

THE DISCOVERY OF THE EMPTY TOMB

SCRIPTURE

It was very early on the first day of the week and still dark, when Mary of Magdala came to the tomb. She saw that the stone had been moved away from the tomb and came running to Simon Peter and the other disciple, the one Jesus loved. 'They have taken the Lord out of the tomb' she said 'and we don't know where they have put him.'

So Peter set out with the other disciple to go to the tomb. They ran together, but the other disciple, running faster than Peter, reached the tomb first; he bent down and saw the linen cloths lying on the ground, but did not go in. Simon Peter who was following now came up, went right into the tomb, saw the linen cloths on the ground, and also the cloth that had been over his head; this was not with the linen cloths but rolled up in a place by itself. Then the other disciple who had reached the tomb first also went in; he saw and he believed. Till this moment they had failed to understand the teaching of scripture, that he must rise from the dead. The disciples then went home again.

JOHN 20.1–10

THE RESURRECTION

Something is green in the house
of a sudden:
all the morning I finger the windows,
revealing the moisture, the heartbeat that rises
   through stone,

and later, in the stillness after Mass,
I guess what it might have been
to discover the tomb:
the empty linen printed with a stain

of presence, like a broken chrysalid,
where something has struggled loose, through
   remembrance and pain,
and the angel, a handsbreadth away,
in the blood-scented shade,
a breathless, impossible being, diverting my gaze
from that which is risen, the living, unnameable God.

JOHN BURNSIDE

MEDITATION

Peter and John running, their hearts thrilling with the news Mary of Magdala has brought. Two more different men could hardly be found, but both are one in their love for the slain Messiah and in the uncertainty and excitement of this moment.

Peter the rock on which the church would be built – impetuous, active, enthusiastic. At times badly mistaken but his faults generous and well-intentioned.

John the beloved disciple – quieter, more reflective, profound and intuitive. Certainly more cautious than his companion!

Peter we can see as the representative of the institutional church, John that of the mystical way that continues to attract and inspire so many within and without that church.

Both so different and both needing the other. Representative not of two ways to God but of two aspects of the one way. Initially brought together by Jesus himself and here the more united in the dawning realization that the Christ has truly risen from the dead.

These different elements are present to us all – how are they balanced? Can the joy of the Risen Lord bring healing and unity to us as well?

PRAYER

Soul of Christ, sanctify me
Body of Christ, save me
Blood of Christ, inebriate me
Water from the side of Christ, wash me
Passion of Christ, strengthen me
O good Jesu, hear me
Within thy wounds hide me
Permit me not to be separated from thee
From the wicked foe defend me
At the hour of my death call me
And bid me come to thee
That with thy saints I may praise thee
For ever and ever. Amen.

ANIMA CHRISTI, ANON.

STATION II

THE ANGEL SPEAKS TO THE WOMEN

THE ANGEL SPEAKS TO THE WOMEN

SCRIPTURE

As they stood there not knowing what to think, two men in brilliant clothes suddenly appeared at their side. Terrified, the women lowered their eyes. But the two men said to them, 'Why look among the dead for someone who is alive? He is not here; he has risen. Remember what he told you when he was still in Galilee: that the son of man had to be handed over into the power of sinful men and be crucified, and rise again on the third day.' And they remembered his words.

LUKE 24.4–8

HER FACE

Love affords wonder
Because it gives us the courage/liberty
to go inside and see who we are really …

MAYA ANGELOU

The woman rolls away
　　stones from our tombs.
　　The silence of the grave
　　is broken.
Some of us
have been told to keep quiet,
hold our tongues,
convinced we have no mouths,
incapable of shaping words
because none would be believed.
It was forbidden to reveal family
secrets, not polite to disrupt the conspiracy,
uncomfortable. Dangerous.
People would die.
Our mothers abandoned. It would be our
fault. We buried
our voices
deeper into the puckers of self-blame.
　　But the woman at the empty tomb
　　with the throat full of grace
　　tells us truth.
　　She writes stories within her skin,
　　carries their songs in her long body,
　　her rhythms leap into our soul's lining.
　　We cannot keep still.

Her face is familiar,
　　radiates all colors of the rainbow.
Her words breaking like light,
　　a bird's full wing,
　　allure a sunrise,
　　wind on free blue water.

The tombs of silence
are emptied. She informs us
that death cannot detain us,
she loves even me and she and he
and we. Her face
is familiar
　　the face of a woman who laughs
　　the one who calls each of us by name.
　　She who brings fruit to the asylum, singing to misfits.
　　The woman who takes nothing from her journey,
　　she who marches for peace, all freedoms, liberating
　　the children.
　　She who does not tolerate brutality.
　　The one who writes poetry for all of a nation.
Language is released
that all understand.
　　'Love affords wonder … ' Maya Angelou says.
We are arranging our faces.
Our mouths bloom with orchids and simple words,
elegant words.

Hope surrounds us.

JANICE MIRIKITANI

MEDITATION

The angel gives us certainty and hope and courage. At last we hear, and can know with absolute certainty, 'The Lord has risen indeed'.

We are reminded how forgetful we can be of all we have already received: the past, all the clues it gives, the messages it offers, the evidence of graces poured out. All there is that can contribute creatively to any situation in the present.

We are challenged too: 'Why look among the dead …'. How at times we cling to what is moribund, sterile and hopeless simply because it is safe, habitual or what is expected.

But enough for now: can you really take it in, and can you let your mouth bloom, your heart sing?

PRAYER

O Lord our God, grant us grace to desire you with a whole heart, so that desiring you we may seek and find you; and so finding you, may love you; and loving you, may hate those sins which separate us from you, for the sake of Jesus Christ.

ST ANSELM (1033–1109)

STATION III

CHRIST APPEARS TO THE VIRGIN MARY

CHRIST APPEARS TO THE VIRGIN MARY

QUOTATION

'Here it is how, after Christ had risen body and soul from the sepulchre, he appears to his blessed mother.' She had brought him to birth, raised him, and had stood by him throughout the passion. Now he wants to share with her the joy of his resurrection.

ST IGNATIUS LOYOLA (THE SPIRITUAL EXERCISES 219)

EASTER

Most glorious Lord of life, that on this day
Didst make thy triumph over death and sin;
And having harrowed hell didst bring away
Captivity thence captive, us to win:
This joyous day, dear Lord, with joy begin,
And grant that we for whom thou didest die
being with thy dear blood clean washed from sin,
May live forever in felicity.
And that thy love we weighing worthily,
May likewise love you for the same again;
And for thy sake that all like dear didst buy,
With love may one another entertain.
So let us love, dear love, like as we ought.
Love is the lesson which the Lord us taught.

EDMUND SPENSER (1552–99)

MEDITATION

You are invited to witness the joy of another, another who has a greater claim than you or I. One who shares our call and has participated in the same gifts, but who has responded with more generosity and greater freedom.

In Acts 1.3 we read that Jesus appeared to many other people, and many writers, from the early Fathers of the church to Ignatius Loyola, could not imagine that our Lord did not appear to his beloved mother. Some might argue that it is a spiritual and psychological necessity, others might propound simple supernatural good sense. Either way it is a personal and intimate moment as mother and child, who somehow are also creature and creator, come together and are reunited.

Love incarnate returns to its source and the bearer of that love rejoices. We who are later witnesses to that greater joy, are reminded that our own joy is not solitary, not unique, not even deserved. It is part of a greater pattern, a greater gift, and all creation will find its place in it.

Perhaps too it is a joy to share?

Thou shalt know him when he comes,
not by any din of drums-
nor the vantage of airs-
nor by anything he wears.
Neither by his crown-
nor his gown.
For his presence known shall be
by the holy harmony
that his coming makes in you.

FIFTEENTH CENTURY, ANON.

PRAYER

Almighty God, give us wisdom to perceive you, intellect to understand you, diligence to seek you, patience to wait for you, eyes to behold you, a heart to meditate upon you, and life to proclaim you, through the power of the spirit of our Lord Jesus Christ.

ATTRIBUTED TO ST BENEDICT (480–553)

STATION IV

CHRIST APPEARS TO MARY MAGDALENE

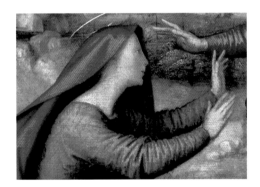

CHRIST APPEARS TO MARY MAGDALENE

SCRIPTURE

Meanwhile Mary stayed outside near the tomb, weeping. Then, still weeping, she stooped to look inside, and saw two angels in white sitting where the body of Jesus had been, one at the head, the other at the feet. They said, 'Woman, why are you weeping?' 'They have taken my Lord away' she replied 'and I don't know where they have put him.' As she said this she turned round and saw Jesus standing there, though she did not recognise him. Jesus said, 'Woman, why are you weeping? Who are you looking for?' Supposing him to be the gardener, she said, 'Sir, if you have taken him away, tell me where you have put him, and I will go and remove him.' Jesus said, 'Mary!' She knew him then and said to him in Hebrew, 'Rabbuni!' – which means Master. Jesus said to her, 'Do not cling to me, because I have not yet ascended to the Father. But go and find the brothers, and tell them: I am ascending to my Father and your Father, to my God and your God.' So Mary of Magdala went and told the disciples that she had seen the Lord and that he had said these things to her.

JOHN 20.11–18

A Psalm for Easter

VII

On the morning of the third day
love rose up early
inside the tomb.

Love breathed in my ear
and lifted me.
Love set me upright.

Then love rolled the stone away.
Then love opened my mouth.
Then love made me rise.

And I, who had died in this life
was born back into it.
I, who had died, was risen.

And she whom I had been searching for
was there. She was with me.
She was love's body:

alive
made whole again
in me.

MICHELE ROBERTS

MEDITATION

Mary Magdalene is such a type and pattern for so many of us: so occupied by cares and concerns, so hampered by clung-to grief or self-obsession, we miss the Lord calling to us. Not just calling to us, but calling to us by name. Our name.

Surely all else is irrelevant? Human frailty fades into insignificance, sin is blotted out, forgotten. Those concerns with what is past are gone, finished. All that is, is now, in the present and the risen Lord calling me by my name.

There is nothing to cling to but this calling, not even the person of Jesus himself. Out of it may come a sending, a sending with the news to others. But for the moment it all comes down to this: the risen Lord calling me by my name.

How does he say your name? What tone does he use?

PRAYER

Thou who art over us,
Thou who art one of us,
Thou who art also within us,
May all see thee in me also,
May I prepare the way for thee,
May I thank thee for all that shall
fall to my lot.
May I also not forget the needs of others,
Keep me in thy love
As thou wouldest that all should be
kept in mine.
May everything in this my being
be directed to thy glory
And may I never despair.
For I am under thy hand,
And in thee is all power and goodness.

Give me a pure heart – that I may see thee,
A humble heart – that I may hear thee,
A heart of love – that I may serve thee,
A heart of faith – that I may abide in thee.

DAG HAMMARSKJOLD (1905–61)

THE DENIAL OF THE RESURRECTION

THE DENIAL OF THE RESURRECTION

SCRIPTURE

While they were on their way, some of the guard went off into the city to tell the chief priests all that had happened. These held a meeting with the elders and, after some discussion, handed a considerable sum of money to the soldiers with these instructions, 'This is what you must say, "His disciples came during the night and stole him away while we were asleep". And should the governor come to hear of this, we undertake to put things right with him ourselves and to see that you do not get into any trouble.' The soldiers took the money and carried out their instructions, and to this day this is the story among the Jews.

MATTHEW 28.11–15

In Portugal, 1912

And will they cast the altars down,
Scatter the chalice, crush the bread?
In field, in village and in town
He hides an unregarded head;

Waits in the corn-lands far and near,
Bright in His sun, dark in His frost,
Sweet in the vine, ripe in the ear-
Lonely unconsecrated Host.

In ambush at the merry board,
The Victim lurks unsacrificed;
The mill conceals the harvest's Lord,
The wine-press holds the unbidden Christ.

ALICE MEYNELL (1847–1922)

PRAYER

O Christ our brother
In spite of our weakness and betrayal
you desire our love.
Give us grace to accept your forgiveness,
that we may be raised to new life in you.

MEDITATION

The forces that threaten are now before us.
Bribery, lying, deceit all are brought into play,
corrupting both the soldiers and those who seek
to hide the truth.

What dangers lurk? What within or without will
seek to undermine the truth? What may challenge
the full power of the Resurrection?
What denies us and our society the possibilities
and potential of this transforming love? Where do
faith, hope and trust fall short?

Many forces whisper here, counselling expediency,
telling us that the end justifies the means, bringing
out the doubt and fear that will eat away at the
integrity we do have, the love that we already
know. Evil has many masks and it is surely best to
know them.

Whatever frailty or uncertainty hamper our lives,
we also need to know that ultimately nothing lies
outside the power and joy of the Resurrection,
nothing detracts from our call to be an Easter
people, and nothing will stop our Alleluya song.

But in the meantime, what should our knowledge
of ourselves and of our Lord bid us beware of?

STATION VI

THE ROAD TO EMMAUS

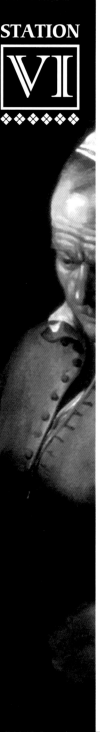

THE ROAD TO EMMAUS

SCRIPTURE

That very same day, two of them were on their way to a village called Emmaus, seven miles from Jerusalem, and they were talking together about all that had happened. Now as they talked this over, Jesus himself came up and walked by their side; but something prevented them from recognising him. He said to them, 'What matters are you discussing as you walk along?' They stopped short, their faces downcast.

Then one of them, called Cleopas, answered him, 'You must be the only person staying in Jerusalem who does not know the things that have been happening there these last few days'. 'What things?' he asked. 'All about Jesus of Nazareth' they answered 'who proved he was a great prophet by the things he said and did in the sight of God and of the whole people; and how our chief priests and our leaders handed him over to be sentenced to death, and had him crucified. Our own hope had been that he would be the one to set Israel free. And this is not all: two whole days have gone by since it all happened; and some women from our group have astounded us: they went to the tomb in the early morning, and when they did not find the body, they came back to tell us they had seen a vision of angels who declared he was alive. Some of our friends went to the tomb and found everything exactly as the women had reported, but of him they saw nothing.'

Then he said to them, 'You foolish men! So slow to believe the full message of the prophets! Was it not ordained that the Christ should suffer and so enter into his glory?' Then, starting with Moses and going through all the prophets, he explained to them the passages throughout the scriptures that were about himself.

When they drew near to the village to which they were going, he made as if to go on; but they pressed him to stay with them. 'It is nearly evening' they said 'and the day is almost over.' So he went in to stay with them. Now while he was with them at table, he took the bread and said the blessing; then he broke it and handed it to them. And their eyes were opened and they recognised him; but he had vanished from their sight. Then they said to each other, 'Did not our hearts burn within us as he talked to us on the road and explained the scriptures to us?'

They set out that instant and returned to Jerusalem. There they found the Eleven assembled together with their companions, who said to them,
'Yes, it is true. The Lord has risen and has appeared to Simon.' Then they told their story of what had happened on the road and how they had recognised him at the breaking of bread.

LUKE 24.13–35

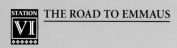

Darest Thou Now O Soul

Darest thou now O soul,
Walk out with me toward the unknown region,
Where neither ground is for the feet nor any path
   to follow?

No map there, nor guide,
Nor voice sounding, nor touch of human hand,
Nor face with blooming flesh, nor lips, nor eyes,
   are in that land.

I know it not O soul,
Nor dost thou, all is a blank before us,
All waits undream'd of in that region, that
   inaccessible land.

Till when the ties loosen,
All but the ties eternal, Time and Space,
Nor darkness, gravitation, sense, nor any bounds
   bounding us.

Then we burst forth, we float,
In Time and Space O soul, prepared for them,
Equal, equipt at last, (O joy! O fruit of all!) them
   to fulfil O soul.

WALT WHITMAN (1819–92)

PRAYER

Set our hearts on fire with love to you,
O Christ our God,
that in its flame we may love you
with all our heart, mind, soul and strength,
and our neighbour as ourselves.
So that, in all things
keeping your commandments,
we may glorify you
as the giver of all good gifts.

EASTERN ORTHODOX CHURCH KONTAKION

MEDITATION

Why is this story so well loved? There are, of course, many resonances that aspects of it have with myth and fairy tale. But there is, too, the reassurance it continues to offer us – even when we do not recognize him Jesus comes and walks with us. He helps to explain, and when he does reveal himself it is in the simplest and humblest way – in the breaking of the bread.

There is, of course, risk in this. It implies we will need to put all our trust and hope in Jesus, even when we cannot see or feel his presence. The disciples were not strangers to uncertainty or danger, before or after the resurrection, and we cannot expect things to be different for us. So this joy may mean going into the unknown, and almost certainly it will mean seeing and doing things differently.

But in this story, as in every Eucharist, we can touch and taste and draw strength from the union of simplicity and profundity, the companionship and revelation that Jesus offers. We can experience daily and weekly the amazing miracle of the scriptures expounded, bread broken and Jesus revealed as the Risen Lord of the universe.

So how can our hearts not burn within us? Our senses not thrill?

STATION VII

CHRIST APPEARS TO THE DISCIPLES

CHRIST APPEARS TO THE DISCIPLES

SCRIPTURE

In the evening of that same day, the first day of the week, the doors were closed in the room where the disciples were, for fear of the Jews. Jesus came and stood among them. He said to them, 'Peace be with you', and showed them his hands and his side. The disciples were filled with joy when they saw the Lord, and he said to them again, 'Peace be with you'.

JOHN 20.19 21A

In Salutation to the Eternal Peace

Men say the world is full of fear and hate,
And all life's ripening harvest-fields await
The restless sickle of relentless fate.

But I, sweet Soul, rejoice that I was born,
When from the climbing terraces of corn
I watch the golden orioles of Thy morn.

What care I for the world's desire and pride,
Who know the silver wings that gleam and glide,
The homing pigeons of Thine eventide?

What care I for the world's loud weariness,
Who dream in twilight granaries Thou dost bless
With delicate sheaves of mellow silences?

Say, shall I heed dull presages of doom,
Or dread the rumoured loneliness and gloom,
The mute and mythic terror of the tomb?

For my glad heart is drunk and drenched with
Thee,
O inmost wine of living ecstasy!
O intimate essence of eternity!

SAROJINI NAYADU

MEDITATION

So the gift of peace is added to the gift of joy. Both suffusing,
possessing ourselves, our souls and bodies, our hearts and minds.
Embracing, harmonizing, integrating all as they flood into our depths.

We can never be the same again.

This is transforming love at work within us that we in our turn
may transform the world in which we live.

How can we ever be the same again?

PRAYER

O Lord, calm the waves of this heart; calm its tempest! Calm yourself,
O my soul, so that the divine can act in you! Calm yourself, O my soul,
so that God is able to repose in you, so that his peace may cover you!
Yes, Father in heaven, often have we found that the world cannot give
us peace. O but make us feel that you are able to give peace. Let us
know the truth of your promise: that the whole world may not be
able to take away your peace.

SØREN KIERKEGAARD (1813–55)

STATION VIII

CHRIST APPEARS TO THOMAS

STATION
VIII

CHRIST APPEARS TO THOMAS

SCRIPTURE

Thomas, called the Twin, who was one of the Twelve, was not with them when Jesus came. When the disciples said, 'We have seen the Lord', he answered, 'Unless I see the holes that the nails made in his hands and can put my finger into the holes they made, and unless I can put my hand into his side, I refuse to believe'. Eight days later the disciples were in the house again and Thomas was with them. The doors were closed, but Jesus came in and stood among them. 'Peace be with you' he said. Then he spoke to Thomas, 'Put your finger here; look, here are my hands. Give me your hand; put it into my side. Doubt no longer but believe.' Thomas replied, 'My Lord and my God!' Jesus said to him:

'You believe because you can see me.
Happy are those who have not seen and yet believe.'

JOHN 20.24–29

THE AIRY CHRIST

After reading Dr Rieu's translation of St Mark's Gospel

Who is this that comes in splendour, coming from the blazing East?
This is he we had not thought of, this is he the airy Christ.

Airy, in an airy manner in an airy parkland walking,
Others take him by the hand, lead him, do the talking.

But the Form, the airy One, frowns an airy frown,
What they say he knows must be, but he looks aloofly down,

Looks aloofly at his feet, looks aloofly at his hands,
Knows they must, as prophets say, nailed be to wooden bands.

As he knows the words he sings, that he sings so happily
Must be changed to working laws, yet sings he ceaselessly.

Those who truly hear the voice, the words, the happy song,
Never shall need working laws to keep from doing wrong.

Deaf men will pretend sometimes they hear the song, the words,
And make excuse to sin extremely; this will be absurd.

Heed it not. Whatever foolish men may do the song is cried
For those who hear, and the sweet singer does not care that he was
  crucified.

For he does not wish that men should love him more than anything
Because he died; he only wishes they would hear him sing.

STEVIE SMITH

MEDITATION

Doubt.

Doubt, no doubt, has played its part on our journey, perhaps at times continues to do so. We can share Thomas' need for certainty and desire for assurance, but it will at times make us miss the point or lead us to settling for something less than might have been.

Even so, if we are here, it is because on some level at least we believe though we have not seen, that in spite of our deafness we have caught something of the song. Doubt in this Gospel story leads to a different sort of encounter with Jesus, and so faith and doubt, in their different ways, can both lead to God.

Doubt without hope would be a different matter, for it can become inward-looking and selfish, but doubt with a desire for answers and a willingness to struggle or challenge can still lead to growth and transformation.

What can we do with our doubts and uncertainties?

PRAYER

O Christ our Saviour, Son of the Father, crucified and risen, grant to us the faith which doubts not your presence, trusts where it cannot see, rests at all times in your love and mercy and rejoices in the example you have set before us, both now and for ever.

AFTER DAVID SILK

STATION IX

THE APPEARANCE ON THE SHORE OF GALILEE

THE APPEARANCE ON THE SHORE OF GALILEE

SCRIPTURE

Later on, Jesus showed himself again to the disciples. It was by the Sea of Tiberias, and it happened like this: Simon Peter, Thomas called the Twin, Nathanael from Cana in Galilee, the sons of Zebedee and two more of his disciples were together. Simon Peter said, 'I'm going fishing'. They replied, 'We'll come with you'. They went out and got into the boat but caught nothing that night.

It was light by now and there stood Jesus on the shore, though the disciples did not realise that it was Jesus. Jesus called out, 'Have you caught anything, friends?' And when they answered, 'No', he said, 'Throw the net out to starboard and you'll find something'. So they dropped the net, and there were so many fish that they could not haul it in. The disciple Jesus loved said to Peter, 'It is the Lord'. At these words 'It is the Lord', Simon Peter, who had practically nothing on, wrapped his cloak round him and jumped into the water. The other disciples came on in the boat, towing the net and the fish; they were only about a hundred yards from land.

As soon as they came ashore they saw that there was some bread there, and a charcoal fire with fish cooking on it. Jesus said, 'Bring some of the fish you have just caught'. Simon Peter went aboard and dragged the net to the shore, full of big fish, one hundred and fifty-three of them; in spite of there being so many the net was not broken. Jesus said them, 'Come and have breakfast'. None of the disciples was bold enough to ask, 'Who are you?'; they knew quite well it was the Lord. Jesus then stepped forward, took the bread and gave it to them, and the same with the fish. This was the third time that Jesus showed himself to the disciples after rising from the dead.

JOHN 21.1–14

THREATENED WITH RESURRECTION

Accompany us then on this vigil
and you will know what it is to dream!
You will then know
how marvelous it is
to live threatened with Resurrection!

To dream awake,
to keep watch asleep,
to live while dying
and to already know oneself
resurrected!

JULIA ESQUIVAL

MEDITATION

The abundance of the catch, the passionate nature of Peter's impetuous act and Jesus' continued hospitality are all key here. All revealing to us as well something of the realm of grace.

For the Kingdom of God that is promised us is abundant, celebratory, creative and generous and we are invited both to help bring all this about and to share and rejoice in the results.

Yet to respond generously and fully to the presence of the risen Lord may not always seem sensible or practical. It may mean bidding farewell to certainty and safety.

So this is to live threatened by resurrection. Living without some of the old securities. But really perhaps living for the first time.

Would that be possible?

PRAYER

O Lord, you have warned us that you will require much of those to whom much is given. May we, who enjoy so rich an inheritance of faith, work together the more fruitfully, by our prayers, our labours and our gifts, to share with those who do not know you what we so plentifully enjoy.

FIFTH CENTURY, ANON.

STATION X

THE QUESTIONS TO PETER

THE QUESTIONS TO PETER

SCRIPTURE

After the meal Jesus said to Simon Peter, 'Simon son of John, do you love me more than these others do?' He answered, 'Yes Lord, you know I love you'. Jesus said to him, 'Feed my lambs'. A second time he said to him, 'Simon son of John, do you love me?' He replied, 'Yes, Lord, you know I love you'. Jesus said to him, 'Look after my sheep'. Then he said to him a third time, 'Simon son of John, do you love me?' Peter was upset that he asked him the third time, 'Do you love me?' and said, 'Lord, you know everything; you know I love you'. Jesus said to him, 'Feed my sheep.

'I tell you most solemnly,
when you were young
you put on your own belt
and walked where you liked;
but when you grow old
you will stretch out your hands,
and somebody else will put a belt round you
and take you where you would rather not go.'

In these words he indicated the kind of death by which Peter would give glory to God. After this he said, 'Follow me'.

JOHN 21.15–19

MEDITATION

We see here another aspect of Jesus' graciousness – the three questions mirroring Peter's earlier threefold denial, leading to a threefold charge. It is a kind of healing and one which both completes and initiates. Betrayal and failure are acknowledged, accepted and set aside once and for all, while the commission to shepherd the flock is firmly and clearly put in their place.

God's call and our frailty are not thus worlds apart or even in opposition. Our weakness can only increase our dependence on God and the extent of God's call or commission to us will be in direct relation to our openness and vulnerability.

We see here Jesus' sensitivity and compassion, speaking the words that heal and make whole. What has been our failure and betrayal? Can we dare to be open and vulnerable to God? Can we let Jesus' compassion bring greenness to our shrivelled hearts?

THE FLOWER

Who would have thought my shrivelled heart
Could have recovered greenness? It was gone
Quite underground, as flowers depart
To feed their mother-root when they have blown;
where they together
All the hard weather,
Dead to the world, keep house unknown.

These are thy wonders, Lord of Power,
Killing and quickning, bringing down to hell
And up to heaven in an hour;
Making a chiming of a passing-bell.
We say amiss,
This or that is:
Thy word is all, if we could but spell.

GEORGE HERBERT (1593–1633)

PRAYER

O Lord and Saviour Jesus Christ, Word of the
everlasting Father, you have borne our griefs and
carried the burden of our weakness. Renew by your
Spirit the gifts of healing in your Church, and send
forth your disciples again to proclaim the good news
of your Kingdom, to the cure of the sick and the
relief of your suffering children, to the praise and
glory of your holy name.

LITURGY OF ST MARK

STATION XI

THE APPEARANCE ON THE MOUNTAIN

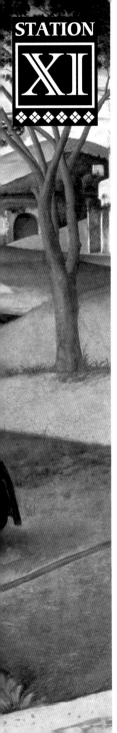

THE APPEARANCE ON THE MOUNTAIN

SCRIPTURE

Meanwhile the eleven disciples set out for Galilee, to the mountain where Jesus had arranged to meet them. When they saw him they fell down before him, though some hesitated. Jesus came up and spoke to them. He said, 'All authority in heaven and on earth has been given to me. Go, therefore, make disciples of all the nations; baptise them in the name of the Father and of the Son and of the Holy Spirit, and teach them to observe all the commands I gave you. And know that I am with you always; yes, to the end of time.'

MATTHEW 28.16–20

THE BEATIFIC VISION

Then Bernard smiled at me, that I should gaze
   But I had gazed already; caught the view,
Faced the unfathomable ray of rays
   Which to itself and by itself is true.

Then was my vision mightier than man's speech;
   Speech snapt before it like a flying spell;
And memory and all that time can teach
   Before that splendid outrage failed and fell.

As when one dreameth and remembereth not
   Waking, what were his pleasures or his pains,
With every feature of the dream forgot,
   The printed passion of the dream remains:-

Even such am I; within whose thoughts resides
   No picture of that sight or any part
Nor any memory: in whom abides
   Only a happiness within the heart,

A secret happiness that soaks the heart
   As hills are soaked by slow unsealing snow,
Or secret as that wind without a chart
   Whereon did the wild leaves of Sibyl go.

O light uplifted from all mortal knowing,
   Send back a little of that glimpse of thee,
That of its glory I may kindle glowing
   One tiny spark for all men yet to be.

G. K. CHESTERTON

MEDITATION

Jesus' final words to his disciples embrace the fullness of Christian endeavour. A life lived in harmony with God, exploring and expressing the joy of the resurrection, must be a life of sharing our good news with others.

And this commissioning of the apostles is not just about bearing witness to others but also being open to the continuing conversion of ourselves. Yet while these must be our task and goal, it is one we share with all other Christian people. Nor is the outcome in any doubt, for Christ is with us in everything, to the end of our days.

Does any part of you yet hesitate?

PRAYER

O Lord, who has taught us that to gain the whole world and to lose ourselves is great folly, grant us the grace so to lose ourselves that we may truly find ourselves anew in the life of grace, and so to forget ourselves that we may be remembered in your Kingdom.

REINHOLD NIEBUHR (1892–1971)

STATION XII

THE REVELATION TO ST PAUL

THE REVELATION TO ST PAUL

SCRIPTURE

Suddenly, while he was travelling to Damascus and just before he reached the city, there came a light from heaven all around him. He fell to the ground, and then he heard a voice saying, 'Saul, Saul, why are you persecuting me?' 'Who are you, Lord?' he asked, and the voice answered, 'I am Jesus, and you are persecuting me. Get up now and go into the city, and you will be told what you have to do.' The men travelling with Saul stood there speechless, for though they heard the voice they could see no one. Saul got up from the ground, but even with his eyes wide open he could see nothing at all, and they had to lead him into Damascus by the hand. For three days he was without sight, and took neither food nor drink.

ACTS 9.3–9

A BETTER RESURRECTION

I have no wit, no words, no tears;
   My heart within me like a stone
Is numbed too much for hopes or fears;
   Look right, look left, I dwell alone;
I lift mine eyes, but dimmed with grief
   No everlasting hills I see;
My life is in the falling leaf:
    O Jesus, quicken me.

My life is like a faded leaf,
   My harvest dwindled to a husk;
Truly my life is void and brief
   And tedious in the barren dusk;
My life is like a frozen thing,
   No bud nor greenness can I see:
Yet rise it shall – the sap of Spring;
    O Jesus, rise in me.

My life is like a broken bowl,
   A broken bowl that cannot hold
One drop of water for my soul
   Or cordial in the searching cold;
Cast in the fire the perished thing,
   Melt and remould it, till it be
A royal cup for Him my King:
    O Jesus, drink of me.

CHRISTINA GEORGINA ROSSETTI (1830–94)

MEDITATION

St Paul, writing himself of this occasion in one of his letters to the Corinthians, says 'and last of all he appeared to me too; it was as though I was born when no one expected it' (1 Corinthians 15.8).

Significantly, he makes no distinction between this appearance of the risen Lord and those that took place immediately after that first Easter morning, for Jesus is beyond time and the encounter with him is always in the now, in the eternal present.

So last of all Jesus appears to us, to you and me. We too are part of the unfolding story of Jesus' revelation to his creation, the continuing gospel.

We can see how this meeting changed Paul's life, the miracle thereby that Jesus brought about in his life. What may he yet do in yours and mine?

PRAYER

Late have I loved you, O beauty ever ancient,
ever new!
Late have I loved you
And behold, you were within, and I without, and
without I sought you.
And deformed, I ran after those forms of beauty you
have made.
You were with me, and I was not with you; those
things held me back from you,
things whose only being was to be in you.
You called; you cried; and you broke
through my deafness.
You sparkled; you shone; and you chased
away my blindness.
You became fragrant; and I inhaled and
sighed for you.
I tasted, and now hunger and thirst for you.
You touched me; and now I burn for your embrace.

ST AUGUSTINE OF HIPPO (354–430)

STATION

XIII

THE ASCENSION

THE ASCENSION

SCRIPTURE

Now having met together, they asked him, 'Lord, has the time come? Are you going to restore the kingdom to Israel?' He replied, 'It is not for you to know times or dates that the Father has decided by his own authority, but you will receive power when the Holy Spirit comes on you, and you will be my witnesses not only in Jerusalem but throughout Judaea and Samaria, and indeed to the ends of the earth'.

As he said this he was lifted up while they looked on, and a cloud took him from their sight. They were still staring into the sky when suddenly two men in white were standing near them and they said, 'Why are you men from Galilee standing here looking into the sky? Jesus who has been taken up from you into heaven, this same Jesus will come back in the same way as you have seen him go there.'

ACTS 1.6–11

STILL I RISE

Out of the huts of history's shame
I rise
Up from a past that's rooted in pain
I rise
I'm a black ocean, leaping and wide,
Welling and swelling I bear in the tide.

Leaving behind nights of terror and fear
I rise
Into a daybreak that wondrously clear
I rise
Bringing the gifts that my ancestors gave,
I am the dream and hope of the slave.
I rise
I rise
I rise.

MAYA ANGELOU

MEDITATION

This moment of farewell is not an end but a culmination of all that has gone before. From the Angel's first greeting to Mary, from the wonder of Jesus' birth, all things having been building to this point: the return of Jesus to his Father and the reuniting of all it means to be human with the Divine Godhead.

All that rich imagery in the Bible comes to fruition here. The tragic effects of the Fall in Eden are reversed and the prodigal world finds its way back home. Finally we find the place prepared for us at the heavenly banquet and at last we can see clearly the face of our God.

And not only is this a completion of so much, it also initiates the new age of life in the Spirit. However attached we have become to the person of Jesus this reminds us of the need to share in the fullness of God, Father, Son and Spirit, that our own fullness may be realized.

Rejoice in that fullness that even now is coming to birth in you!

THE ASCENSION

Lift up your heads, great gates, and sing,
Now Glory comes, and Glory's King:
Now by your high all-golden way
The fairer Heaven comes home to-day.

Hark! now the gates are ope, and hear
The tune of each triumphant sphere;

Where every Angel as he sings
Keeps time with his applauding wings,
And makes Heaven's loftiest roof rebound
The echoes of the noble sound.

JOSEPH BEAUMONT (1615–99)

PRAYER
TAKE, LORD, AND RECEIVE

Take, Lord, and receive all my liberty, my memory, my understanding, and my entire will – all that I have and possess. You have given all to me: To you, Lord, I return it. Everything is yours; do with it according to your will. Give me only your love and your grace, for this is sufficient for me.

ST IGNATIUS LOYOLA (1491–1556)

STATION

XIV

Pentecost

*P*ENTECOST

SCRIPTURE

When Pentecost day came round, they had all met in one room, when suddenly they heard what sounded like a powerful wind from heaven, the noise of which filled the entire house in which they were sitting; and something appeared to them that seemed like tongues of fire; these separated and came to rest on the head of each of them. They were all filled with the Holy Spirit, and began to speak foreign languages as the Spirit gave them the gift of speech.

Now there were devout men living in Jerusalem from every nation under heaven, and at this sound they all assembled, each one bewildered to hear these men speaking in his own language. They were amazed and astonished. 'Surely' they said 'all these men speaking are Galileans? How does it happen that each of us hears them in his own native language? Parthians, Medes and Elamites; people from Mesopotamia, Judaea and Cappadocia, Pontus and Asia, Phrygia and Pamphylia, Egypt and the parts of Libya around Cyrene; as well as visitors from Rome – Jews and proselytes alike – Cretans and Arabs; we hear them preaching in our own language about the marvels of God.'

ACTS 2.1–11

MEDITATION

All receive the Holy Spirit and all receive it in their own language, in their own way. It is present to us all by our creation and redemption, it is guaranteed by our membership of the Church and is enhanced by our communal life, and it is ours individually, uniquely and personally.

This account recalls, of course, the Old Testament story of the Tower of Babel. In the Spirit the children of God now find unity and mutual understanding to be their calling, and their faith is to be a place of acceptance and hope.

We therefore are gifted with the Spirit and by it given the power to become all that we have been created to be, all that even now we are called to be in Christ. Whatever jack, joke, patch or potsherd we experience ourselves to be, we are also immortal diamond and in the end that is all that matters. Immortal diamond.

That Nature is a Heraclitean Fire and the Comfort of the Resurrection

Cloud-puffball, torn tufts, tossed pillows
   flaunt forth, then chevy on an air-
built thoroughfare: heaven-roysterers, in gay-gangs
   they throng: they glitter in marches.
Down roughcast, down dazzling whitewash, wher-
   ever an elm arches,
Shivelights and shadowtackle in long lashes lace, lance,
   and pair.
Delightfully the bright wind boisterous ropes,
   wrestles, beats earth bare
Of yestertempest's creases; in pool and rut peel
   parches
Squandering ooze to squeezed dough, crust, dust;
   stanches, starches
Squadroned masks and manmarks treadmire toil there
Footfretted in it. Million-fueled, nature's bonfire
   burns on.
But quench her bonniest, dearest to her, her clearest-
   selved spark
Man, how fast his firedint, his mark on mind, is gone!
Both are in an unfathomable, all is in an enormous dark

Drowned. O pity and indignation! Manshape, that
   shone
Sheer off, disseveral, a star, death blots black out;
   nor mark
     Is any of him at all so stark
But vastness blurs and time beats level. Enough! the
   Resurrection,

A heart's-clarion! Away grief's gasping, joyless days,
   dejection.
     Across my foundering deck shone
A beacon, an eternal beam. Flesh fade, and mortal
   trash
Fall to the residuary worm; world's wildfire, leave but
   ash:
     In a flash, at a trumpet crash,
I am all at once what Christ is, since he was what I am,
   and
This Jack, joke, poor potsherd, patch, matchwood,
   immortal diamond,
     Is immortal diamond.

GERARD MANLEY HOPKINS

PRAYER

Grant, O merciful Father, that your
divine Spirit may enlighten, inflame,
and cleanse our hearts; that we may
be penetrated with your heavenly
dew, and made fruitful in all things.
We ask this for you live and reign,
Father, Son and Holy Spirit, ever one
God, world without end.

FROM THE GOLDEN MANUAL